Dear Parents,

 P9-DNK-711

Welcome to the Scholastic Reader series. We have taken over 80 years of experience with teachers, parents, and children and put it into a program that is designed to match your child's interests and skills.

Level 1—Short sentences and stories made up of words kids can sound out using their phonics skills and words that are important to remember.

Level 2—Longer sentences and stories with words kids need to know and new "big" words that they will want to know.

Level 3—From sentences to paragraphs to longer stories, these books have large "chunks" of texts and are made up of a rich vocabulary.

Level 4—First chapter books with more words and fewer pictures.

It is important that children learn to read well enough to succeed in school and beyond. Here are ideas for reading this book with your child:

- Look at the book together. Encourage your child to read the title and make a prediction about the story.
- Read the book together. Encourage your child to sound out words when appropriate. When your child struggles, you can help by providing the word.
- Encourage your child to retell the story. This is a great way to check for comprehension.
- Have your child take the fluency test on the last page to check progress.

Scholastic Readers are designed to support your child's efforts to learn how to read at every age and every stage. Enjoy helping your child learn to read and love to read.

—Francie Alexander
Chief Education Officer
Scholastic Education

For Jeffrey, with much love
— M.B. and G.B.

Special thanks to Charles S. Miller
of the Cheyenne Mountain Zoological Park
for his expertise

Photography credits:

Cover: Daniel J. Cox/STONE; page 1: Dominique Braud/Dembinsky Photo Associates; pages 3 and 26: Carl R. Sams, II/Jean F. Stoick/Dembinsky Photo Associates; page 4: Stan Osolinski/Dembinsky Photo Associates; pages 5 and 40: John Warden/STONE; page 6: Mark J. Thomas/Dembinsky Photo Associates; pages 7-9: Erwin & Peggy Bauer; pages 10-11: Mark J. Thomas/Dembinsky Photo Associates; page 12: J&K Hollingsworth/U.S. Fish and Wildlife Service; page 13: Carl R. Sams, II/Dembinsky Photo Associates; pages 14-15: Claudia Adams/Dembinsky Photo Associates; page 16: Lynn Rogers/Peter Arnold, Inc.; pages 17-18: Erwin & Peggy Bauer; page 19: Carl R. Sams, II/Jean F. Stoick/Dembinsky Photo Associates; page 20: Dominique Braud/Dembinsky Photo Associates; page 22: Claudia Adams/Dembinsky Photo Associates; page 23: S.J. Krasemann/Peter Arnold, Inc.; page 25: Carl R. Sams, II/Peter Arnold, Inc.; pages 27-30: Erwin & Peggy Bauer; page 31: Alaska Stock Images; page 33: Erwin & Peggy Bauer; page 34: Mark J. Thomas/Dembinsky Photo Associates; page 35: Engraving after Gustave Doré/The Granger Collection; page 36: Erwin & Peggy Bauer; page 39: Pedro Ramirez, Jr./U.S. Fish and Wildlife Service.

No part of this publication may be reproduced in whole or in part, or stored in a retrieval system, or transmitted in any form or by any means, electronic, mechanical, photocopying, recording, or otherwise, without written permission of the publisher. For information regarding permission, write to Scholastic Inc., Attention: Permissions Department, 557 Broadway, New York, NY 10012.

Text copyright © 2002 by Melvin & Gilda Berger.
Activities copyright © 2003 Scholastic Inc.

All rights reserved. Published by Scholastic Inc.
SCHOLASTIC, CARTWHEEL BOOKS, and associated logos are trademarks and/or registered trademarks of Scholastic Inc.

Library of Congress Cataloging-in-Publication Data is available.

ISBN 0-439-20167-5

10 9 8 7 6 5   08 09 10 11 12 13/0

Printed in the U.S.A.   23
First printing, January 2002

HOWL!

A Book About Wolves

by Melvin & Gilda Berger

Scholastic Reader — Level 3

Cartwheel
·B·O·O·K·S·®

SCHOLASTIC INC.
New York Toronto London Auckland Sydney
Mexico City New Delhi Hong Kong Buenos Aires

CHAPTER 1
Wild and Wonderful

The wolf points its muzzle up toward the sky.
It begins to howl.
AH-WOOOO!
The eerie sound rings out across the land.
You can hear it for miles around.

Why does the wolf howl?
No one is sure.
But experts think it howls —
• to bring the pack together before a hunt.
• to keep in touch with other wolves.
• to warn enemies to stay away.
• because howling feels good!

Wolves love to howl.

They howl all hours of the day.

They howl all seasons of the year.

A wolf by itself howls for less than

a minute at a time.

But often other wolves join in.

Then they have a longer — and louder —

howling session!

Wolves are one of the largest members
of the dog family.
And like dogs, wolves are friendly,
smart, and playful.
But wolves are wilder than dogs.
And wolves are amazing hunters.

Wolves often hunt animals much larger than themselves.
They hunt deer, elk, moose, caribou, and wild sheep.
They live by catching and eating these animals.

Wolves are very well-built for hunting.
They have strong muscles and long legs.
They can run for hours without getting tired.

Long legs also help in other ways.
Wolves can leap through deep snow while chasing an animal.
And they can swim across rivers and streams.

Like dogs, wolves walk on their toes, not on the soles of their feet.
This lets wolves move very fast.

Running wolves can reach speeds
of 30 miles an hour!
And they can easily leap over
big rocks and logs.

Wolves have powerful jaws and very sharp teeth.

A wolf's teeth are like a dog's teeth — except that they are bigger and stronger.

- The four sharp, long fangs in front grab and hold the prey.
- The sharp teeth along the sides cut through tough flesh.
- The back teeth crush bones.
- And the small teeth in front pick meat off the bones.

Besides sharp teeth, the wolf has an
amazing sense of smell.
Scientists say it is about 100 times
better than that of humans.
Wolves can smell a deer from over
a mile away!

The wolf's hearing is also excellent.
One time a scientist howled like a wolf.
Four miles away some wolves heard
his howl.
And they joined in!

Did you know that wolves can move
their ears?
They can turn them forward or
to the sides.
This tells wolves the direction of any sound.
Then they can follow it.

When hunting, wolves depend mostly
on smell and hearing.
But they also see very well.
They're especially good at spotting
anything that moves.

Most wolves are gray.

But the color is not always the same.

Wolves can be almost any shade

from white to black.

Often, their fur is a mixture of shades.

Dark-colored wolves are called

timber wolves.

They have pointed ears and short hair.

Timber wolves live mostly in thick forests.

Their dark furry coats make them hard

to see among the trees.

Some wolves have light or white fur.
They are called **tundra** or **Arctic
wolves**.
You can spot tundra wolves by their
rounded ears and longer hair.

Tundra wolves live in very snowy areas.
Their long, thick, white furry coats
keep them warm.
And their light color helps them blend
in with the snow.

Red wolves have red or brown fur.
They are smaller than most other wolves.
Some say they look more like coyotes
than wolves.
Large numbers of red wolves used to live
in the fields and forests of the southern
United States.
Today very few are left.

All wolves hunt animals for food.
The wolf's strong body, cutting teeth,
and sharp senses fit it for this job.
So does its way of life.

CHAPTER 2
A Wolf's Life

Wolves live in **packs**, or groups, of wolves.
Each pack has 7 to 20 members.
They are usually a mother and a father,
their young, and some other adults.

Pack members take care of each other.
They help one another hunt, travel,
and feed.
Together they fight off enemies.

Wolves are good parents.
In the spring, the wolf mother goes into
an underground den.

She gives birth to about 5 or 6 babies.
They are called **pups**.
The pups look like little gray bundles
of fur.

At first the pups are tiny and helpless.
They can't see or hear.
The mother wolf feeds them milk from
her body.
The pups grow very fast.

At about two weeks of age, the pups'
eyes open.
They learn how to walk.
One by one, they come out of the den.
Soon they're playing and tumbling
on the ground.

Around this time, the pups start to
eat meat.
They get it from adults after a hunt.
The adults eat the flesh of the animal
they have caught.
Then they head back to the young.
The pups rush up and lick the adults' jaws.
This makes the adults cough up the food
they swallowed.
The pups lap it up.
It is their first taste of meat!

By ten weeks of age, the pups leave
the den.
They start to live with the rest of the pack.
But they're not yet ready to hunt.

While the adults look for food, the young
wolves play.
All summer long the pups tumble and roll
on the ground with one another.
They pounce and fight.
They chase insects and small animals.
Through play, the pups learn to be good
hunters.

Young wolves play two games that
you know.
One game is tag.
They chase each other around.
The other game is hide-and-seek.
One wolf hides and jumps out when the
other wolves come close.

When playing, a few pups stand out from the others.
Usually they are the biggest and strongest.
The other pups give way to them.

The "top" pups grow up to become the leaders of the pack.
They are called the **alpha** (AL-fah) **wolves**.
All the wolves of the pack follow the alpha wolves.

Adult wolves play, too.

To show they want to play they —

• bend down low.

• put their front legs flat on the ground.

• wag their tails.

Wolves use sounds to communicate.

Whines tell the pups to stop playing roughly.

Barks signal surprise or danger.

Growls express anger.

And soft squeaks seem to say, "Everything's okay."

At six months, wolves are old enough
to hunt.
The whole pack runs down its prey.
But only the older wolves make the kill.

The young hunt with the pack until they
are about two years old.
By then they are full-grown adults.
Some wolves stay with the pack.
Others leave to find mates and start
new packs.

Sometimes an alpha wolf and a
pack wolf quarrel.
The two wolves growl at each other.
They bare their teeth.
It looks as if each is about to attack.

But the alpha wolf quickly shows its rank.
It raises its head.
It moves its ears forward.

It holds its tail up in the air.
And it glares at the other wolf.

The pack wolf backs off.
It lowers its body and tucks its tail
between its legs.
Sometimes it rolls on to its back to
show that it gives up.

The quarrel is over.
Neither wolf is hurt.
The alpha wolf trots away — head, ears,
and tail held high.

CHAPTER 3
The Big Hunt

The alpha wolves decide when it's time
to hunt.
They gather the pack together.
And they lead the way.

Wolves hunt large prey because
they live in packs.
There must be enough meat
for everyone.
But how do the wolves find their prey?
How do they kill animals larger and
stronger than themselves?

Wolves usually find their prey
by sniffing the air.
An alpha wolf picks up the
prey's smell.
It points its head in that direction.

All the animals stand alert.
Their eyes, ears, and noses face
toward the prey.
The alpha wolves give the signal.
And the wolves head off that way.

Sometimes wolves spot their prey
by accident.
The pack of wolves may be
wandering through a forest.
They come to a clearing.
An elk is drinking at a small pond.
The alpha wolves lead the pack
toward the elk.

Other times, wolves discover fresh animal
tracks in mud or snow.
The lead wolves follow the tracks.
The others follow behind in a single file.

The pack moves toward the animal.
They make sure the wind is blowing
in their faces.
This way they can smell the animal.
But it cannot smell them.

When the pack gets close to the prey,
the wolves spread out.
Working together, they rush in to attack.

Sometimes the prey fights back.
It slashes at the wolves with its
powerful hooves.
It butts them with its pointy antlers.
The wolves turn and flee.

Sometimes the prey runs off.
The wolves give chase.

Moose and other large animals can
run very fast.
They often outrun the wolves.
In fact, wolves only catch about one
out of every ten moose they hunt!

But sometimes the pack nabs the prey.

One wolf bites the animal's side.
Another goes for its hind part.
Others stab its neck and nose.
Soon the animal is bleeding from
its wounds.
It becomes weak, falls to the ground,
and dies.

The alpha wolves eat first.
The rest wait their turn.
Each wolf gulps down as much as
20 pounds of meat.
But it may not feed again for two weeks!

Wolves can eat healthy or sick animals.
But sick animals are easier to catch.
So, wolves often eat them.
This stops the sickness from spreading.
It makes animal herds bigger and
healthier.

Luckily, the wolves do not get sick themselves.

Sometimes the wolves' victims are old and weak.
Killing them leaves more food for younger, stronger animals.
This, too, helps the herd to grow.

From time to time a wolf leaves
the pack.
It becomes a lone wolf.
Such wolves live and hunt
by themselves.

A lone wolf can't snag big animals.
So it mostly hunts small prey,
such as mice, rabbits, squirrels,
and beavers.
In time, the lone wolf may find a mate,
have babies, and start a new pack.

CHAPTER 4
Wolves and You

Are you afraid of wolves?

Many people are.

They grow up reading *Little Red Riding Hood* and *The Three Little Pigs*.

They hear the tale of *Peter and the Wolf*.

And they believe what they read and hear.

Stories often make wolves seem sly and nasty.

These wolves trick people or animals.

They kill or hurt their victims.

But the truth is very different.

Wolves only kill to eat.

They hardly ever attack people!

In fact, it is usually the other way around.

Humans kill wolves!

Long ago, wolves lived throughout North America.

The Native Americans admired them.

Many wanted to be as strong and smart

as wolves. They wore wolf skins to get some of the wolves' powers. They wore wolf masks to be as wise as the wolves.

Over the years, many people settled
in places where the wolves lived
and hunted.
These men and women shot many
of the wolves' usual prey.
They turned the woods and fields into
farms and ranches.

Gradually, the wolves found fewer wild
animals to hunt.
With not enough to eat, the wolves began
to prey on farm animals.
They attacked ranchers' sheep and cattle.
They raided farmers' coops and fed on
their chickens.

Of course, this made the ranchers and
farmers very angry.
They shot, trapped, or poisoned the
wolves.
The number of wolves dropped way down.

Today wolves live in just a few parts
of North America.
Only a few thousand can be found in the
entire United States.
The red wolf is nearly extinct.

But times are changing.
People now realize that wolves are not
evil killers.
They know that farm animals and humans
are not part of a wolf's diet.

Now there is a new worry about wolves.
So many have been killed that soon they
may all go the way of the dinosaurs.
Wolves may become extinct.
They all may disappear from our planet.

A few years ago, the government decided
to help save the wolves.
They rounded up several wolves in Canada.

And they brought the wolves to Yellowstone National Park in the U.S. Then they set them free.

These wolves are now growing and multiplying.
They are finding food in Yellowstone and other national parks.
Very few of them are eating livestock.

Slowly, the wolves are coming back.
You can hear them howling —
AH-WOOOO! — in more and
more places.
What a thrilling sound!